Hello Sunshine,

My name is Maisy. I am here to help you change into a better person by following different challenges.

This is one of the activity challenges that would help you succeed in life.

It is time for you to change into a better person.

Wish you all the best!

Enjoy

21 Days to say "I love you" without saying it. You will build a solid relationship and be more loving, kind, and thoughtful towards your significant other.

Spend 60 minutes completing the daily challenge.

Once you've completed the task, tick the relevant day's checkbox.

Day 1	◯	Day 11	◯	Day 21	◯
Day 2	◯	Day 12	◯		
Day 3	◯	Day 13	◯		
Day 4	◯	Day 14	◯		
Day 5	◯	Day 15	◯		
Day 6	◯	Day 16	◯		
Day 7	◯	Day 17	◯		
Day 8	◯	Day 18	◯		
Day 9	◯	Day 19	◯		
Day 10	◯	Day 20	◯		

Day 1

Make a list of the things you love about your family members, partner, and friend.

Day 2

Plan a surprise of a special day and keep it remembered by writing it down.

Day 3

Tell your family, partner, or friend that you love them at an unexpected time.

Write down what happened

Day 4

Share a fear you felt about your past with any member.

Write how you skipped it.

Day 5

Share a memory you have about any of your family members, or your partner

Day 6

Send your family
member or partner
a romantic
morning text or
audio

How did you feel?

Day 7

Thank your family members or partner for something today

How did you feel?

Day 8

Surprise your family member or partner with something good.

How did you feel?

Day 9

Share a goal you
want to achieve,
either with a
family member or
partner.

How did you feel?

Day 10

Give either a family member or partner a compliement

How did you feel?

Day 11

Plan a weekend give away with a family member

How did you feel?

Day 12

Look at old pictures, either with a family member or your partner

How did you feel?

Day 13

Reminisce about when you first met, either with your partner or your friend.

How did you feel?

Day 14

Make a bucket list of the best memories with either your family member or your partner

Day 15

Pick a random word and start a deep conversation with either a family member or your partner.

How did you feel?

Day 16

Do a puzzle with either a family member or your partner

How did you feel?

Day 17

Write a letter to either your family member or your partner and hide it for them.

Draft

Day 18

Do something with either your family member or partner that they enjoy, like cooking together.

How did you feel?

Day 19

Make either your family member or partner a favourite treat

How did you feel?

Day 20

Tell either your family member or partner something you remember they like.

How did you feel?

Day 21

Give either your family member or partner a hug when they're not expecting it.

How did you feel?

Write down the change you found after 21 days

Congratulations

Congratulations

You have completed the tasks provided. I am proud of you!

I still have other challenges that you can enjoy and have a new habit change in your life.

Maisy